eave shakings
North Hills Monthly Magazine 2017

Villa Vuoto Publications
Copyright © 2017

ISBN: 1 979549 52 4
EAN-13: 978 1 979549 52 3
First Edition
628

Text and illustrations by
Matthew Schlueb

For the student of architecture,
the following stories speak to the essential in architecture.

May the imagery within this collection of ponderings,
brought about by a paper written as a graduate student,
inspire minds of future architects in the handling of space.

VillaVuoto
2017.01.05

significance

Tables - every house has one, in fact most houses have two. One for daily meals, a second for dining over formal occasions. Is it really necessary to have two tables? Both are rarely used at the same time. Why can't one table be enough?

Maybe two tables are needed because they serve two very different functions. And, those functions cannot be served on the same form of table. Sure, some households manage to get by on a single table, my own house included. However, I would argue when this is the case, something is missing or at the very least, not addressed.

The two tables, found in the typical suburban American house, have many common characteristics. The daily table practical in proximity to family activities and routines, the dining table set aside in a controlled and decoratively stage room, speaking more to the family's dreams than the pleasures of a good meal.

In fact, these dining tables are appointed with straight lines and right angles throughout, in both the surface and the surrounding chairs, seat, back, weave. This rectangular language permeates the air with a stiffness, a weighting of the moment, to elevate occasions marked by the gathering of extended family or friends.

By contrast, the tables we use daily have a rounded nature, edges eased, softer. Why do we prefer this circular form for our daily use? Is it merely a physical thing, lending better to the vocabulary of our bodies, the ergonomics of our limbs? Or could it be more than that? Speaking to a relationship we once had, long ago, when the forms and spaces we inhabited as an earlier people were round? Does this table we choose for our daily habits, resonate on a much deeper level, comforting us precisely because of its shape, fulfilling a faint, nearly unperceivable cry from our past?

What is the significance of such things? How has this difference between tables gone unnoticed? It is a small detail, but not an insignificant one, as this pattern exists almost universally in every home. Something is going on here, these tables are witness to something in our nature, more than just happenstance.

Single table houses, make no distinction between meals, each one is significant, living in the moment. Single table houses are often smaller houses and one may say it is the lack of space for a second table. But, I would say those who live in the moment, appreciate the value of every single object they encounter on a daily basis, desire fewer things by choice. Having less, what remains, is enhanced.

In a larger house, there is certainly space for more things. One has the ability to separate functional needs into multiple tables. But, it is not merely a matter of excess or convenience, rather an organizational device signifying a fundamental difference in perception.

In two table houses, there is a desire to hold certain meals at a higher importance from all the rest, a differentiation stating, not all meals are created equal. And, by placing these moments onto a second table, reserved only for these rare occasions, we are stating a commitment to hierarchies. Valuing certain things over others.

This may be why after a dozen years living in a single table house, I am planning to add a second table this year. In a space isolated from the rest of the house, a second table resides in command of its own room, defining the space, rather than defined by it. Our house is currently configured around a single table and so, we live our lives one meal at a time, the table is shaped by our doings. But soon, the structure of our house will change, physically and metaphysically, by the addition of a second table. It is the difference between reaction and intention.

For the past couple months, my wife has been arranging broken tiles on a table, a mosaic of color and shape. Much thought has gone into a surface laid by hand and in doing so, a meaningfulness has been created of what was once an ordinary table.

Maybe this is how we preserve a single table mindfulness in a two table house. The investment of time, whether puzzling shards of tile or breaking daily bread together, infuses a moment and the table on which it is shared with its own hierarchy, each one different, but no less significant.

Jan 01, 2017 03:01PM, Published by North Hills Monthly Magazine, Categories: Home+Garden, Today
http://www.northhillsmonthly.com/2017/01/01/132042/what-is-the-significance-of-a-table-

thresholds

This week marks the start of another lunar year, the Chinese New Year, which began with the new moon this past Saturday. With any moment that signals a transition into something new, there is usually some form of celebration. At the very least, there is a marker placed, to indicate something has changed, that things are no longer what they were.

In a house, there are many of these and in the architectural trade, we call them thresholds. The term derives from *thresh* (to separate seeds from grain) and *tread* (to step on), a stepping onto a separate condition. In a pragmatic sense, we think of thresholds as that strip of wood, metal or stone on the floor in a doorway, facilitating a change in flooring material between one room and the next. But to architects, it has more meaning than a mere construction detail to resolve material differences.

We accentuate thresholds, call attention to and raise their stature, the front door is the most prominent case. Crossing the threshold into a house is a deliberate act, a significant moment when we have entered a new realm, from the outside world into the inside, a personal space we have been invited into. By doing so for the first time, our perspective of the homeowner changes, our mental image of them now includes all the things we find inside their home, their character deepens to include a layering of artifacts housing a lifetime of experiences. Once we pass through that threshold, we can no longer return to a previous state, our relationship has changed and the front door to a house celebrates that moment, sets the stage.

In my own house, the front door has what we refer to in the trade as a no-step, accessible threshold, the floor inside the house is level with the ground outside. So, the physical transition is subtle, but the effect is there nonetheless. In case you might miss it, I placed a second threshold within the house, between the living room and kitchen. At that point there is a step up into the kitchen. During construction of the house, I laid a couple pieces of 4x4 cut-offs as a makeshift step. My plasterer teased me at the time, saying that I would never get around to replacing it with a formal, finished step.

He was right, although, a couple years ago my wife tiled over it with broken mosaics, adding color and a playful spirit to compliment the house. The step finally felt as if it was meant to be, the threshold was properly delineated.

Aside from a functional purpose, this step does something more for the house. As in many homes, most people enter through the back door, in our case the kitchen door. So, the point of reference into the open space of our ground floor is from the kitchen and when one moves to the living room, they step down, a lowering into. Combined with the living room walls that lean in, there is a definite sense of enclosure, a burrowing down, nestling into a cozy place.

By contrast, for those that enter the house through the front door, the step takes you up into the kitchen, elevating, as if placed on a pedestal, when something is clearly not by chance but with intent. Entering into our kitchen, one gets the sense of arriving at the heart of our home.

The difference between these two experiences, the sensations defining these two rooms, are in a large part the result of this step, a threshold that changes perception by the direction of movement through. In the end, that is really the point of a threshold, to mark the location where perspectives change, to signal an envelope has been reached with irreversible implications. Not as in a tipping point, rather a milestone. Where space makes a palpable shift, the atmosphere takes on a different feel. For an architect, this is one of the devices we use to shape space, create experiential architecture. The articulations of a threshold may vary, a step or no step, sometimes simply the narrowing of a constricted passage. No matter the case, this is the toolset in which we play.

With a new year upon us, what the future holds is unknown. However, one thing always for certain, life is in continuous change. It may very well be the driving force behind all living things and the reason why we humans celebrate its thresholds.

Jan 30, 2017 07:45PM, Published by North Hills Monthly Magazine, Categories: Home+Garden, Today
http://www.northhillsmonthly.com/2017/01/30/134274/the-thresholds-of-a-house

grounding

Housing and clothing share a common purpose, both strive to give shelter from the elements, the natural world. Ever since humans took their first steps inside or clothed their bodies, we enhanced our comfort, made our environment more tolerable. Facilitated by a distancing, a separation, leaving the world outside.

However by doing so, we soon forget the warmth of the sun on a bare back or the sense of grounding felt by the earth giving way to the imprint of bare feet. If we happen to find ourselves outdoors without shoes, we rarely step off asphalt or concrete onto the soil, for fear of getting dirty. This tactile existence to the natural world is avoided, replaced by the firm, clean, controlled floors of our home.

An awareness of gravity is disguised by all these trappings. The ground floor of our homes still rooted in the earth, maintains a relation to the landscape. But, when we ascend the stairs to our bedrooms on a second floor, atop a bed further elevated in the air, the realm of clouds and dreams, we are attempting to defy gravity, by leaving the ground below.

When dining, working or unwinding at the end of the day, we sit on chairs elevating us. Most of daily life is disconnected, so it is no surprise to find the cultures that do maintain a connection are rooted in the ancient practice of sitting directly on the ground. The separations we create through proximity or by physical constructs have an impact on us, alter our experiences, influence our perceptions.

For example, the shoes that we wear and the surfaces on which we step affect the way we walk. Every woman remembers the first time she put on a pair of heals. We step cautiously when footing is unsure, the sensitivity of our toes heightens to a level more accustomed to our fingers, as we feel our way across rocky terrain. A late night trip to the bathroom, half asleep in the dark, may not be in tune, but we quickly become aware when something unexpected is stumbled over in our path.

In the bathroom of my own house, I tried to address this dislocation of the body from the ground. A mosaic of broken tiles cover the floor and turn up the walls, in a rounded transition that pays homage to Antoni Gaudí - an architect from the turn of last century, who perfected the study of gravity by creating inverted architectural models to calculate the naturally forming profiles in the catenary curves of his buildings.

However, it is the irregular shard edges of the broken tiles on the floor, varying in the tilt and level of their setting, that enhance an awareness under foot. In considering such a floor, my first thought and concern was possible injury to bare feet. However after the grouting was complete, I was pleasantly surprised by the invigorating feel, a sort of foot massage at the start of each day.

We insulate our feet from the ground by layers of socks and shoes, just as we do our bodies from the outdoors by layers of clothing and the walls of our home. The ground becomes a projection beyond our feet, as socks and shoes become an extension of our body. When we walk, we feel with the bottom of our shoes, not our toes and by doing so, our perception is something altogether different than a perception with bare feet.

Our homes do the same, the ground is projected through the elevated floors on which we step. A stability is transferred to us through the flooring under foot. We are reminded of its presence in the weight of our body, drawn to the floor, a seat or bed. The continual fatigue of muscles and bones to resist the ever present force of gravity. We construct these furnishings and structures, a layering to provide separation, offering relief, escape from the relentless demands of the natural world.

However, as in my own bathroom, I prefer that these layers we are in contact with routinely, to be surfaces that speak to the gravity of the situation. A door knob or cabinet pull with an unmistakable weight when taken in hand, expresses a sense of solidity, does not let us forget we are a participating in a world that is real, one that necessitates an interface.

A house filled with surfaces that accentuate the tactile experience, keeps us present in the moment as we go about our living. This weight of materials, layer upon layer, remind us that we are still biological creatures, interacting with our surroundings physically. We seek a sensual authenticity, in an ever increasing artificial existence.

And, it is through the materiality of these fixtures and surfaces we touch, that we may find reassurance. It is a subtle thing, gravity is not seen or heard, it operates directly on the body, subliminal. But, it is there nonetheless and relentless in a pursuit to wear us down.

The houses we inhabit and clothing we wear, silently isolate us from a connection deep in our evolutionary history. These things we have created bring bodily comforts, but can weather away a metaphysical fullness dependent on a grounding within our environment. Yet, with some thoughtful consideration, the right materials can restore a meaningful tactility, a genuine connection, grounding.

Mar 03, 2017 09:15AM, Published by North Hills Monthly Magazine, Categories: Home+Garden, Today
http://www.northhillsmonthly.com/2017/03/03/136444/the-weight-of-materials

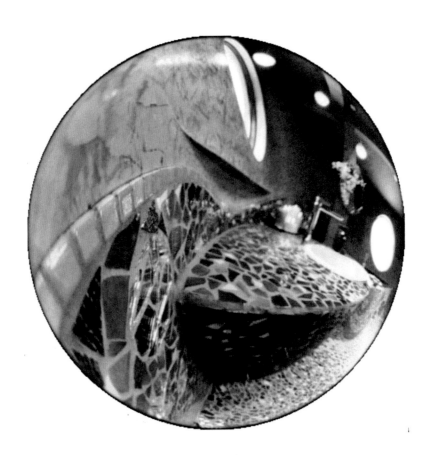

circularity

Last month I spoke at Pittsburgh's 26th PechaKucha Night, a gathering of creative minds to share their latest ideas. I presented a talk titled, "Are We the Last Architects?", which questioned the roll and impacts of big data and generative design software in the architectural profession. In particular, my concern that in short order, the automated construction site transformed by 3D printers taking direction from Building Information Modeling (BIM) software optimized to generate the most efficient structures in material, energy, and functional uses, may mark the end of architects in the design process.

In an artificial intelligence world where automated systems surpass human abilities in nearly every measure, if not all, what is the role of an architect? Green building practices, the sourcing and implementation of environmentally friendly building materials and their application in the construction sequence, has in recent years become the dominant role the architectural profession has defined for itself, rebranding as LEED Architects, Leadership in Energy and Environmental Design.

The "green" issue is important and in my opinion vital to our future. However, as I argued in my presentation, that role will be done far more effectively and accurately by machine learning computing utilizing predictive analytics, than in the hands of an architect acting traditionally on trial and error. This will not happen overnight, there will be a transition period integrating the insights and experience of humans in a partnership with computers. But, now that big data has been introduced into the process, it won't be long before human involvement is no longer needed, viewed as a hindrance slowing things down and ultimately a liability.

This brings me to the subject of creativity, what I believe is at the heart of the human condition - our ability to leap, attaining new ground by leaping into realms unknown, the creative act. And in the leap, as the leap, a questioning happens, where existing conditions are no longer taken as givens, alternatives are considered, a search for a better way of doing things compels this creative leap. This speaks to our fullest measure as human beings, it is here that we find our passions and dreams.

As architects, like every creative profession, we are all about the questions. Yet, if there is to be a next generation of architects, they will be asking 'Why' we build, not 'How' we build. The houses in which we dwell will continue to become more energy efficient and flow functionally, however will they fulfill our emotional longings better than the homes we live in today or the past?

This pursuit I placed above all else in creating a home for my own family. I began with a blank sheet of paper, questioning every convention, ruling out no possibility or opportunity. And, with my interest in indigenous architecture, the circular space of early humans, I wondered how living within rectilinear shaped rooms in our modern existence has changed us. Standardization of dimensional building materials and right-angle assembly has certainly aided the mass production of housing. However, has the benefits been across the board (forgive the pun) or maybe, has something been sacrificed, lost in our rush to progress?

In putting pencil to paper, I took the circle as a starting point, an attempt to infuse those properties inherent to circular form, not found within the orthogonal. Windows and doors were made round, as was the layout of space in plan. As a result, every trade during construction, masons and carpenters, plumbers and electricians, had to figure out new ways to install the fixtures and finishes. It was a daily challenge to work against accepted norms, however, everyone who had a hand in the process welcomed the change from the routine, commenting on minds numbed by years of building the same thing over and over.

In this experiment of circular space, not everything was abandoned, it was not merely an exercise for novelty sake. This was an act of creativity, a questioning of conventions and by doing so, coming to understand the reasons why with a greater appreciation and connection. And, isn't this the true nature of exploration? To dig deeper, finding the original purpose of a thing, to see if it still serves that intent and if not, figuring out how it has gone astray. Maybe the houses we build today lost touch precisely because our response to a changing environment did not prioritize the continual human condition.

Despite the shape of the human body, our being is round. Our eyes, the windows to our soul are circular, not just for the pragmatics of capturing light, but more importantly for spiritual reasons. Life is circular metaphorically, as is the cyclical nature of time. Is it any surprise the earth on which we live is a sphere? One might expect the spaces we inhabit would be round too? Well, not surprisingly, they began that way, for tens of thousands of years. Only recently has that changed. Maybe we should be questioning why?

This is what I tried to do with the house my family inhabits and by doing so, found creativity in circular space. When my son puts a ball on the round window sill, delighted to watch it roll back and forth, I am reminded of the unlimited spirit of a child, experimenting without preconceptions to learn about their environment. Maybe this is the answer to our changing times, a future without architects, where homeowners create their own houses. A simple reminder to question and consider something alternative, then the ability to leap into new ground, creativity.

Apr 02, 2017 12:07PM, Published by North Hills Monthly Magazine, Categories: Home+Garden, Advertisers, Today
http://www.northhillsmonthly.com/2017/04/02/138397/the-circular-nature-of-creativity

creativity

Last month I wrote an article about the advancements of technology in home design and the possibility that we may be the last generation with architects. If this is not the case, I proposed human creativity might be the only thing to save the profession. Either way, what does this mean for the future of home design? Or, the homeowner?

The way I see it, creativity varies from person to person, some more creative than others. As an architect, I have developed a creativity spectrum to better understand my clients' comfort level and preferences for the home I help them create.

In general, I believe people fall into one of four groups.

To illustrate, I use a cooking analogy. In the first group, when preparing a dish for a meal, those with little creativity prefer to follow a recipe - exactly. I call this the *script* group, no deviation from a predetermined script. Individuals who want everything spelled out, so the decision-making process is done for them, by a cookbook.

The second group is more creative, they are willing to substitute ingredients for those in the recipe not found in the kitchen. This takes a certain degree of confidence and imagination, to try something not prescribed. It has been my experience, that the vast majority of the population falls into this second group that I call *switch*, willing to switch out a few things when need be.

The third group is more adventurous, they prefer taking the path less traveled. After reading over the recipe, they enjoy experimenting, creating a new variation on the dish with all new ingredients and flavors. The original idea is still there, they have simply shifted the outcome to a dish not found in any cookbook – the *shift* group.

The last group is the most creative of all, creating a dish by simply using the ingredients on hand in the kitchen. Unlike the other three groups that use the recipe to varying degrees, this fourth group does not have a recipe. Consequently, they are not boxed in by preconceived ideas, they are driven by the thrill of creating something unimagined. This is the *scratch* group that starts each exploration from a blank slate.

How does all of this relate to the future of architecture and home design?

As do-it-yourself apps continue to increase in sophistication, enabling homeowners to generate a complete set of building plans for their next addition or home makeover, will the creativity of an architect matter?

As I argued in last month's article, maybe they become outmoded by an automated workplace. Architects at the lower end of the creativity spectrum will likely find themselves out of work before those at the higher end, since *script, switch* and *shift* routines are much easier to automate than *scratch* methods.

In fact, novelty and unexpected discoveries may serve us best in these accelerating times with an uncertain future. And, maybe the kitchen is the best place to taste test such experimentation. Switching out a few ingredients if you tend to follow the recipe, has a temporary consequence - only a meal stands to be ruined.

On the other hand, if you are pleasantly surprised by the risk-taking venture, it might lead to shifting the recipe altogether next time, maybe even starting from scratch. Next thing you know, a new-found spirit for the unknown will spread from cooking in the kitchen to redecorating the kitchen. And, the change in space will influence daily routines, creating a new outlook on life.

The role of an architect is changing and soon homeowners will be empowered by software and smart devices to design their homes without them. Maybe that is the way it should have been from the beginning, people creating their homes for themselves. Because in the end, who knows you better than yourself?

Certainly, there is an expertise to the design and building process that architects have traditionally provided. However, I have always found a certain arrogance to architects designing the way people are to live in their own homes. As an architect, I prefer to approached the process like a concierge, guiding homeowners through the maze of decisions that accompany the transformation of a house.

By studying the way people use their homes or the changes that occur with a growing family, architects acquire objective insights that benefit the average homeowner. And it is here that I believe to be the greatest value of an architect, not in the logistics of code compliance or energy efficiencies in the construction of a house. I welcome the advance of technology taking away those tasks from me, so more focus will be placed on the human condition in the design of space, the habits of habitation, the creation of meaningful place.

These are the things that impact the quality of life, why some houses feel better than others. And, they don't happen by chance. So, as homeowners find themselves fumbling through a newfound role wearing the architectural hat, the architects of tomorrow would do well to become beacons, nudging creativity in homeowners, helping them consider possibilities outside the familiar, to create a home that prepares them for a changing world.

As all of these new technologies infuse our homes with automation, our lifestyles are changing. Daily routines become easier by apps and devices doing the work for us. However, are we prepared for the changing world, the machine learning that is eliminating work in the workplace? Can our homes help us with that?

My own career as an architect is founded on the principle that our environment shapes us as people. That our built environment can do more than make life comfortable, but challenge us to reach our full potential as people. And our homes, the most influential environment we occupy, could take a cue from the creativity we express in the kitchen when preparing a meal.

So, the next time you consider making a change to your home, approach it with the same imagination and experimentation as trying a new dish. Play around with a few new ingredients, maybe a circular window or two thrown in for good measure.

May 01, 2017 08:24AM, Published by North Hills Monthly Magazine, Categories: Home+Garden, Today
http://www.northhillsmonthly.com/2017/05/01/141073/creativity-in-the-kitchen

measure

I often get calls from homeowners in need of an architect to inspect a wall in their house, to determine if it is load bearing and what measures must be taken to remove it. This begs the question, does the average homeowner know what differentiates an architect from a structural engineer?

With over two decades of practice in residential design, one thing I have learned for certain, most homeowners do not know what value an architect can offer in the homebuilding process. However, it is no surprise, since historically the vast majority of homes are constructed without one. So, what is the need for an architect today?

In recent years, more homeowners are interested in green building practices and energy efficiencies. Yet, homeowners often look toward tech devices, such as smart thermostats or surge protectors to monitor and improve their green habits, rather than turning to an architect on such matters.

And in the realm of aesthetics, such as a home makeover to revitalize a dated interior or to add more curb appeal to an exterior, these services are typically perceived as the expertise of a designer, not an architect. Architects are thought to deal with the mechanics of building, their visual contributions are less appreciated.

Over the last couple months, I have made the case that advancements of technology in the design and construction process of homebuilding, automating routine mechanical tasks, is reducing the need for architects. To determine what role architects will have in the future, it might be best to first ask, what is architecture?

This is a question that is often asked of first year students studying architecture. As expected, their answers vary widely. It is no surprise, since centuries of discourse by historians, critics and architects themselves have been unable to reach a consensus on the nature of architecture.

At the turn of last century, sparking the start of a modern movement in architecture, Frank Lloyd Wright touched on the issue when he stated *the usefulness of a house is in the room where life might be lived, not in the form of the house or the material of which it was made - make space for living.*

This I believe is at the heart of architecture. Many consider architecture a form of art, yet it is more than art, as it houses living too, prompting some to call it functional art. Le Corbusier, the pinnacle architect of modern times, differentiated the functional from art as a matter of timelessness. *Certain things serve forever, they are Art.*

So maybe it is the art of function, the way a space is resolved, the relationship of its parts creating a particular flow. A well designed house feels better to live in, much like a tailored suit fitted to your measure can lift spirits and boost self confidence. The translation of physical characteristics into a metaphysical sensation.

This would explain the contemporary vernacular use of the word architecture as it is applied to things outside of the building trade, to describe a system or process. Likewise, the term architect is commonly used outside building, to define the originator or creator of an idea or movement. If an architect creates, then what specifically is this thing called architecture that they create?

Lately, I have been taking portraits of my clients before and after I work with them on the creation (or re-creation) of their home. I do this because I believe the intangible nature of architecture, the influence it has on one's life, is captured best by the changes reflected in the face than on the walls. Architecture reveals the essence of the individual; the individual reveals the essence of Architecture.

And maybe this is at the root of so much confusion and misunderstanding over the role of an architect or more importantly, their value to a homeowner - architecture is not the structure of a building, the visual style, nor the functional use. Yes, it resides in these things and is bound by them, but it is a quality in its own right. This is why it has its own name - architecture.

And the architect, the one who creates it, must attend to this thing called architecture above all else. In the case of a house, an architect can determine if a wall is load bearing, which insulation is more sustainable, or what countertop material holds up best to spills, but the greatest value of an architect is their craft at combining the diverse set of variables that go into a home, in such a way that responds to and enhances the lives of its occupants.

It could be said, that art does this, a beautiful melody or poetic work can inspire. More practically, is the sense of security and comfort provided by a sheltering house any better than savings in a bank account? Further, if architecture is tied to the experiential nature of habitation, would unoccupied buildings, architectural ruins or unbuilt designs be considered architecture?

This last point may be the key to it all - without physically occupying a space, the mind can still wonder and soar through imagination or memory. These things we call architecture exist in our heads, not in the buildings themselves. A mouse that takes refuge in the walls of a house has a very different appreciation for its architectural significance. It is the homeowner (and occasional pet) that the architect designs for.

And most importantly, the designing that an architect does is not in the material transitions and details of the building - these are his toolset. The medium in which an architect designs is the experience a person has with the building. The true creation of an architect is this living that goes on within a building, the life of a building, that is the architecture of a building.

A synthesis of all things concrete and cerebral, culminating in the senses and handled by the architect in a measured way, to resonate with the human condition. In the case of a home, to dwell. And in the dwelling, architecture changes daily life by layering meaning in each experience. This is the nature of architecture and the architect that creates it.

Jun 01, 2017 02:27PM, Published by North Hills Monthly Magazine, Categories: Home+Garden, Today
http://www.northhillsmonthly.com/2017/06/01/145672/the-essence-of-architecture

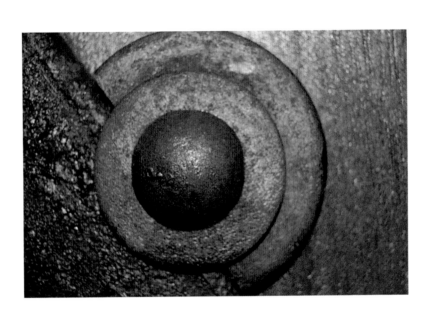

resonance

Recently I made a presentation to a prospective client interested in building a new home. After an initial meeting to learn what their family was looking for in a custom designed and built house, we set a date to meet again four days later, when I would have a preliminary conceptual design ready for their review.

In addition to the usual floor plan and exterior renderings I typically prepare for such a meeting, this time I also brought a pair of Google Cardboard virtual reality goggles, so they could experience the design as if they were standing inside the house, turning their head to look around each room, walking about virtually to take in every view. It was the first time they had put on a VR headset and needless to say, it made quite an impression.

Later that day, while recapping the meeting with an architectural student interning with my studio this summer, she asked how I manage to prepare so much material in such a short amount of time. When she would work on a design in school, she often found herself spending too much time on a particular detail to get it just right, then find herself scrambling to complete the rest of the work in time for the presentations.

I assured her that in architecture, there is never enough time and learning to prioritize the multitude of things, to effectively manage your time is a hard-earned skill that only comes with practice. In the case of my own client presentation, I pointed out several items I wanted to work on, but had to omit. Otherwise, the final presentation would have never been completed in time.

That said, I also commended her attention to detail. The mid-century architect Charles Eames, whose furniture set the standard for precision in design, once stated, *the details are not the details. They make the design.*

There is no denying, one of the common threads within the architectural profession, a trait that nearly every architect practicing today exhibits, is an obsession over the details. Material transitions in particular. For example, how a window jamb meets a plaster wall or the way a bolt engages the hinge of a door. These are the things architects live for, the things that really matter to them when working on the design of a building.

But, are these details what make good architecture?

Last month's article, summed up my exploration into the essence of architecture with a conclusion: Architecture is layering meaning in experience. In the abstract, this makes sense. However, an illustration might serve best to address this issue of detail and how it relates to meaningful experience.

In my twenty plus years of designing homes, I have come across only one homeowner that did not like stone as a building material. Stone is as close to a universal preference if any such thing exists. It is no surprise, as it has been used as a building material ever since humans started building.

Architects think about materials in many different ways. Their structural qualities, durability over time, thermal capacity to moderate temperature, porous nature to absorb and filter water, not to mention the aesthetic beauty of materials visually, tactilely, and acoustically. An architect must consider characteristics like these in the construction of a house, however I believe it is the emotional aspect of a material that is at the heart of architecture.

All of the physical qualities of a material converge together into a perception of that material, subconsciously. This perception is simply a feeling we have, that takes into account all of its physical characteristics like texture, color, warmth, but also metaphorical references such as a romantic ideal or past memory. For example, the stone steps in a backyard might remind of stepping stones in a secret garden from one's childhood home, creating a sense of playful magic and mystery to their current home. All of this happens in an instant - the materials that define the spaces we inhabit, create emotional impressions influencing what we think and feel.

These impressions are the key to designing meaningful spaces, rooms that have a desired feel, a sense of comfort or shelter. I use these to craft an intimacy into a home. Like the fit of a tailored suit, inspiring confidence by how it feels.

Most architects don't get this, they think of building materials only mechanically or aesthetically. However, it is the emotional resonance of a space that defines architecture, the intangibles that are not so easy to put a finger on, but have the greatest influence over how a home becomes a backdrop for life.

And to craft these experiences, which is the true work of an architect, is only done by taking great care in the nuance, the subtleties of perception. Only through an awareness and study of the slightest differences in physical details can we shape the emotive sensations that define our experiences within a space. When an experience is meaningful, resonating deeply in a memorable way, then you have created architecture.

Jul 01, 2017 10:37PM, Published by North Hills Monthly Magazine, Categories: Home+Garden, Advertisers, Today
http://www.northhillsmonthly.com/2017/07/01/148050/architecture-is-made-in-the-details

invisibility

After more than twenty years designing homes, working with dozens of homeowners and countless architectural proposals for commissions, I thought I understood what is desired in a home. As an architect with my own practice, I had always marketed my studio as delivering home designs personalized to a family's unique character.

But, I may have it all wrong.

For the past couple months, this series of articles has been exploring the nature of architecture and I concluded that it is the layering of meaning in experience. Architecture is an interactive thing, resonating individually by one's own involvement with it, colored by past experiences and life memories. In short, it touches on the emotions, which are always dependent on a particular time and place.

Naturally this would lead me to believe the experience of architecture is a very personal endeavor and that the design of a home would be best served when it reflects one's individuality. So, for the last two decades I have been striving to do just that. Trying to find out what makes each family unique, what are their daily habits, their aspirations, their quarks, their tastes.

I believed that a home designed with every detail derived from a family's own story, right down to the slightest nuance, would provide them with the most personalized home, the most enjoyable, the most comfortable.

However, this view may be too simplistic, not taking into account the true depths of the human condition. As my fourteen year old son put it, with no architectural experience, "If a house design is personalized too much, people may feel too exposed, afraid of being judged by their friends knowing more about them."

He may be right. For a home to bring comfort, it must first provide a sense of protection. Protection from judgmental friends, just as much as protection from the rain overhead. And a personalized home, one that conforms to a family, may prove to be uncomfortable for a family that prefers to conform.

This changed everything I thought I knew about the nature of a home. All of my education as an architect, all of the services I thought to be offering beyond the monotony of production houses built for the masses, this was all wrong. There is a reason why houses that look exactly like your neighbor's house sell best on the market, why so few homeowners employ architects to design something new or original.

Individuality is no longer valued in our society. Our social nature and desire to be a part of the group is more important in today's culture. Maybe it has always been that way. The fear of standing out from the crowd overpowers any possible praise for individual achievement. We are content to follow, rather than taking on risk by leading.

The stories we tell each other about the great visionaries of history, are told to fit in, not to be the trailblazer, someone who sets the trends, finding their own path. We are not envious of their spirit, their passion to change the world. We are more afraid of their possible failures, of being left out in the cold by not following accepted standards, protocols, the right way of doing things.

The selfies we take are not forging new grounds, they are taken in places we all go, the sights we have all seen, the preprinted postcards of the digital age. These are the experiences we have, the communal experience, not the individualized. We are about the sharing, not the exploration. And maybe that is best. Why should we strive to be something different, to think differently from the group, to question the way things have always been done? Life is hard enough as it is. Why take on more difficulty?

As a people, we are naturally resistant to change, the status quo is far easier. All of these innovations and advancements in society do not bring pleasure, as much as they bring pain. Always one more thing we must learn to do differently, another burden we must adjust to make smooth again. The newest gadget, this season's latest look, the race to keep up is more exhausting than any reward gained by doing so.

Returning from work at the end of the day, pulling the company car into the garage of the four bedroom, two-and-a-half-bath home is really all we want. A place to retreat, to hide away from the prying eyes scrutinizing our life and choices we have made. In the end, all that is needed of a house is one that disappears, camouflage, provides cover from a social media culture that never sleeps.

As an architect, to design a personalized home that stands out on the block is a disservice, irresponsible, negligent. If I truly understand my client, if I honestly believe to represent their best interests, then invisibility is the most important characteristic to provide comfort in a home.

The architecture of an invisible house is no less intimate, no less meaningful, no less nuanced. In fact, it is quite the opposite – to craft a home that so skillfully blends in to the neighborhood, having just the right accents and trimmings to appear appropriate while not calling too much attention to itself, is not a simple thing. This takes great effort to pull off, sweating the details, surveying the trends and taking care not to be dated.

Architecture hasn't changed, it is still defined by meaningful experience, resonating in a deeply memorable way. I simply misunderstood which experience to craft into a home. I didn't see what was most meaningful and sought after. Then again, an invisible house is not so easy to see.

Jul 31, 2017 08:32PM, Published by North Hills Monthly Magazine, Categories: Home+Garden, Advertisers, Today
http://www.northhillsmonthly.com/2017/07/31/150784/uncomfortable-architecture

entropy

When I work on a renovation or addition with a homeowner, the subject of resale invariably comes up. Most homeowners want to avoid a design decision that would reduce the chances of selling their house or spending money on alterations they will not recoup.

My answer to these questions is typically the same - if they are planning to move out of their house in two or three years, then these issues need to be taken into account. However, if they are not planning to move out for five years or more, I believe resale should be the least of their concerns.

In five years' time, the marketplace changes quite a bit. Trying to predict where it will be or what style will be in fashion is anyone's guess. Even a recently remodeled house will likely have some minor changes made by homeowners moving in, such as painting walls a new color or changing out light fixtures. For these reasons, design decisions made based on one's own tastes are best. So that during the five years or more before reselling, the house can be thoroughly enjoyed.

Why go through the inconveniences of construction for a homeowner that may move in some day? Shouldn't you benefit the most from all the money and effort you spent on the renovations? If materials and fixtures are selected anticipating some buyer's preferences, whose house are you living in? You're merely a temporary guest in the home of a future owner.

Five years ago, a house on the market was more desirable with a big Jacuzzi tub in the master bathroom. Today's buyer however, prefers that the precious square footage in a bathroom is allocated toward increasing the size of the shower. Massaging water jet sprayers have become an active showering experience, no longer valued for rejuvenating in a reclining tub.

Then again, was the master bath whirlpool ever truly used? A new home may be christened by a candlelight soak on the first weekend, but too often it is rarely used again. The pace of modern day life does not afford the time, forgotten the luxury. The tub has become a perpetually empty vessel, holding only imagined experiences.

These are the places we inhabit. We do not meditate submerged in water, we live in 'possibilities' and 'someday doings'. A whirlpool is not a white acrylic tub with polished chrome faucet and knobs. It is a suburban rite of passage to unfulfilled promise, containing our mind more than body.

The objects that fill our houses acquire us, rooms are created for antiquated traditions. The thought of a relaxing soak is the only use for a tub, the actual act of untangling tense muscles is never experienced. The tub provides metaphor, aspirations, fantasy, not device.

The spaces we occupy speak to our emotions, of conservation and safety. Environments crafted to provide insurances, more than possibility. Before a house becomes a home, it is first an investment, a mortgage, a milestone.

Under this measure, a house is not a vehicle for living, life is barely sustained. It is entropic, thinning and dispersing toward invisibility and phantom space. Bathroom tubs that don't hold water, they are human scale vessels disappearing in plain sight.

We are reselling the American Dream and by remodeling the master bath with an empty tub, we are participating in the American experience of living within conventions and expectations. And, by building houses in a culture of resale, designed for the typical buyer, suburbia has become a uniformity in which everything is neither here nor there. Houses without measure.

What is to be done for the homeowner with an independent mind and the conviction to follow their own tastes? Can such a person exist in today's housing climate of quick flips and maximized return on investment? In our race to conformity, appealing to the common pool, the trendsetters and tastemakers seek dissonance to differentiate and find new ground. Any hope for the suburban homeowner is no different.

In the end, when asked about resale, I advise my clients that it is a personal decision which comes down to comfort. Do they draw more pleasure from the idea of a rejuvenating tub or the actual act of drawing a bath? After that question has been considered honestly - understanding why you feel inclined to include a new Jacuzzi in your master bathroom renovation - the question of resale value takes care of itself.

Sep 01, 2017 08:34AM, Published by North Hills Monthly Magazine, Categories: Home+Garden, Today
http://www.northhillsmonthly.com/2017/09/01/153823/don-t-let-resale-value-compromise-home-s-comfort

symbiosis

Lately, I have been working with my two sons, building robots from miniature servos and Arduino boards. Playing around with such things got me thinking that we could automate the kookoo clock in our basement, whose gears and carved wooden bird fell silent years ago. The pendulum motion driven by weighted chains and levers could be wired to operate electronically, powered by the sun if we included a solar cell.

I find it curious, as tools and constructs have advanced over time, technological innovations continue to hold references of the natural world they strive to overcome. The charm of this mechanized clock for example, is not found in the wizardry hidden out of sight inside a small wooden box. Rather, it is the surprise of a bird popping open a door, mimicking the sounds heard in nature. As our lives continue to be filled with more and more artificial things, the romance and longing for a more authentic time only grows.

However, maybe something more than simple sentimentality is at work here. Symbiotic microorganisms inhabit plants and animals, in the case of our own bodies, outnumbering human cells three to one. Referred to as a microbiome, these collective genomes found a way to exploit an environmental niche influencing our health and behavior. In short, at the microscopic scale, they play a crucial role in our interactions with all other lifeforms.

Further, when we leave our house, traces of our microbiome that has exchanged and morphed with other microbiomes in that environment, will remain behind without us. And then when we return, our internal ecosystem recognizes those microbes from our body, sending a signal to our senses, that comforting feeling of home. The sentimentality we experience for a place is in part biologically triggered by our microbiome.

When we step outdoors, our microbiome mixes with the mycorrhizal web of life, the multitude of living things that are in constant interaction and change. We may not notice it consciously, but the sensations we feel within our physical body and mind register this biological exchange. It is the reason a breath of fresh air clears the mind, refreshes the spirit.

Don't believe what your eyes are telling you. All they show is limitation. Look with your understanding, find out what you already know. Our perceptions, feelings, intuitions extend beyond ourselves, they are largely formed by our interactions with the environment on a molecular level, invisible to the naked eye. We couldn't survive without them – literally. The fondness we have for bird songs, compelling us to recreate their calls in a clock, stems from a relationship with birds over centuries, remnants of their microbes mixed in with ours.

Thousands of years ago, when societies formed in collective villages or settlements along trade routes, the first houses were packed tightly together. The desire to be close in proximity, acting as a group against outsiders beyond perimeter walls, defined civilized life. Clustered houses created facade lined streets, concealing families within. Yet, ties to nature were not lost by this new lifestyle – at the heart of each home was an interior courtyard. By each room opening into this outdoor space, household activity remained informed by the natural world.

That is something that has been lost by the modernization of our current homes. Air conditioning has shut the doors and windows to cross breezes, as well as those microbes drifting on the wind. The air we breathe indoors has become stagnant, in fact, studies have found it unhealthier than the air outside. However, a house built with outdoors indoors, a thoughtful insertion, may be just the answer.

If our homes were designed with an open, central courtyard, holding the house together as arms of a pinwheel, the ritual slumber from bedroom to kitchen coffee machine, would require passing outdoors, infusing our senses with crisp morning air, possibly a rain shower or a blanket of snow in the winter. Awoken by just a dozen steps, we would no longer have a need for the weather channel or even the aroma of coffee to start our day. We would reconnect in a way more immediate, more natural, a way that has been lost, forgotten.

Our ancient ancestors found an advantage by living close together, closed in by walls with a roof overhead to keep dry as they slept through the night. Yet, they were also not quite ready to cut ties from a natural world their body and mind had adapted to over generations of symbiotic dependence and connection. We are still not ready today – the boundless possibilities we feel by watching a sunrise or the beauty emoted by a sunset bears witness.

If architectural space is created by layering meaning into each experience, then the emotions we feel that provide meaning and tangible significance, result directly from the dialog we are having with the environment we inhabit, a communication facilitated practically by our microbiome operating on a microscopic scale. And, a home without closed doors, keeping nature's microbes in close proximity, instantly and unfiltered, is the type of environment in which our body and mind were formed, despite a recent move indoors.

You may say it would be crazy to live daily within a house so open and exposed, the added inconvenience of accommodating inclement weather or an uninvited mouse. Such a way of life in today's day and age, one would call kookoo.

Still, our ties to nature are not so strange, even if they have become estranged. Times have changed by our mechanizations and advancements, but why are Bavarians compelled to make clocks with birds popping out from behind doors every hour of the day? Is an automated birdcall their attempt to bring the outdoors in?

I like to think it is a reminder that we are the kookoo, shutting ourselves inside a box behind closed doors. Every so often, we need to take a break and pop outside, call out to the world beyond our birdhouse, then pause for a moment to allow our body and mind to feel the response before returning back in. It is a small thing, but still needed. And, a compromise far more convenient than living in a house without doors.

Oct 01, 2017 11:12AM, Published by North Hills Monthly Magazine, Categories: Home+Garden, Today
http://www.northhillsmonthly.com/2017/10/01/156165/birdcalls-for-home

armatures

What is it about clockmakers, that make them good architects?
Is it their propensity for puzzling, able to fit so many moving
parts into a confined housing? Or maybe, it is their intuitive
sense of timing, crafting mechanisms that come to life in
a measured, predictable way. I like to think it is their
understanding of gears, levers, and pendulums. A good
architect must first know how to build, the sequencing of
materials, each providing a necessary function, assembled in
such a way to make a structure stand.

One of the greatest architects in modern history, was raised a clockmaker. He had no training in buildings when he claimed to know how to construct a dome over the largest cathedral the world had ever seen. 'How could a clockmaker know how to build such a dome?', the city fathers of Florence thought. Their cathedral stood open to the sky for over a century, because no one in Europe knew how to build a dome to span the opening.

It was so large in fact, there was not enough timber available in all of Italy to erect the scaffolding needed to support the masonry until the dome was complete. But, this was Filippo Brunelleschi's genius, the clockmaker figured a way to build a dome without scaffolding, senza armatura, without armature. And today, over five hundred years later, that dome still stands as the largest masonry dome in the world.

He crafted bricks into particular shapes, interlocking them to be self-supporting as they were laid in successive rings, like cogs fitting together in the gears of a clock. Further, he designed the dome in the shape of an upright egg, recognizing that this natural profile transfers all of the weight of a masonry dome directly down, without the need for lateral buttressing. These ideas were revolutionary in construction and changed architecture forever.

In my mind, it was this absence of scaffolding and buttressing that defined him as a true Renaissance architect. Solving problems by finding solutions within the materials of construction, not in the crutches others would add to make things stand up. He dealt directly with the material at hand, eliminating everything else as obstacles.

Too often architects get caught up in the armatures and buttresses, lose sight of what is really going on within a space. It is easy to be distracted by sleek skins and sexy technologies, not giving much thought to the consequence of such design decisions.

The walls we build no longer protect us from what is outside, they are too permanent. In our retreat inside, we have lost touch with the outside - physically. And by doing so, we are more tuned to the tick of a clock, than the call of a bird. The outside world no longer offers us a meditative balance, a healthy exchange, our walls have closed us off.

Not long ago, I crafted a pivot hinge with a 3D printer, that enabled a Dogon granary door to be used for the powder room off our living room. The fabric curtain we had hanging in the opening previously remained, providing some privacy by drawing across the cracks between the door planks leaking light and sightline for peeking eyes. However, complete privacy is absent, since the rectangular door does not fit tight to the irregular curved opening, so the sounds and smells of the bathroom escape.

Naturally, this makes most visitors to our home uncomfortable. It may even play a role in the length of their visits. But, this door experiment was not intended to offend or create discomfort. Rather, it was a tool to study the nuanced dimensions of inhabited space. We take for granted the security behind a closed door, to the point we no longer notice it. Much the way we no longer notice the outdoors.

Using a door that does not close out sights and sounds, makes you more aware of your surroundings, more tuned into your senses. The door may not have the precision of a clock when it comes to closing, but it commands your attention immediately. You notice things you didn't noticed before. How a Spring breeze tickles tree leaves and when sunlight passes through, dances from one branch to the next, changing direction and shifting shadows, bending light.

And maybe, this is the lesson our homes could learn from Filippo - there is a world of sights and sounds out there, that our walls and doors have closed us off from. And by doing so, our eyes no longer see, ears no longer hear. A dulling of the senses, that a permeable house living life more directly, without armatures or obstacles to the tactile world, could restore a sensitivity and symbiosis with the environment we have lost.

Oct 31, 2017 05:18PM, Published by North Hills Monthly Magazine, Categories: Home+Garden, Advertisers, Today
http://www.northhillsmonthly.com/2017/10/31/158920/armatures-and-buttresses

tensiles

It is that time of year, strings of lights emerge from storage boxes, to be strung along roof overhangs, outlining neighborhood houses at night. The air has a festive feel, each gust of cold winter wind swaying these strings, the lights become twinkling stars in the sky.

Hanging holiday lights from the eaves has an additional pleasure for me. It is a chance to channel my inner Shaker propensity for placing things into suspension, to toy with gravity. Architects relish playing with such things and I guess that is why I find myself living inside a house with sloped walls - an excuse to question the most ordinary of things, such as a bookshelf. Suspended in space by cables from the ceiling, out away from the sloping walls, a bookshelf becomes a swing, in tensile dialog with mother earth.

One of my favorite architects, Antoni Gaudí, was a master of gravity, understanding its pull on structures, giving weight to materials. His Catalan creativity utilized an ingenious method of study to isolate and tune this planetary force imposed on buildings. By inverting architectural models upside down, arches became hanging slings, allowing gravity to shape their curvature to the most stable profile, a catenary arch. The same profile used by the Inuit to construct igloos with blocks of ice, to withstand the collapsing weight of compacted snow on top.

Further, Gaudí would tie a series of strings with small weighted bags from the inverted arches, to represent the intersecting points of columns carrying roof loads. Like a mechanical calculating machine, his model of weights and strings would adjust naturally by gravity alone, determining the position and inclination of each structural member, intuitively designed to be in perfect balance with the ground underfoot.

The close of another year reminds us that nothing is permanent, all things change. Even something immense as the planet earth is also temporary. Its surface continually shifting, shaking the foundations of our buildings, mountains rising, ice sheets fracturing. We may wish to live in a world that is fixed, with certainty, where all things are known. However, reality is not, permanence is an illusion.

To compensate, our houses have an appearance of stability, ordered and tidy, a solid roof overhead. So much so, that when something unexpected comes along, something not planned for, it can be quite unsettling. We are reminded that life can be unpredictable, nature is constantly adjusting, reacting, re-centering, ignoring our desires for the contrary.

Maybe our houses need to be more soluble, permeable, allowing the outside in. Could the walls of our homes and the things they house, bring us more in harmony, at ease, with an ever-changing world?

For example, the shower in my own house has a hanging curtain made of glass plates, the result of several factors related to frugality, practicality and my fondness for gravity. While taking a shower, the slightest of movements cause the plates to rattle, the sounds of a wind chime in a soft breeze. It is a subtle thing, however, the experience becomes infused with a sense of fragility, the brevity of a breeze, the transience of a moment.   I may not notice these things as my mind wonders showering, yet my senses are tuned, subconsciously. I am refreshed mentally, beyond just soap and water.

Around the house, I continually seek out ways to create these tensile structures, things within the home that communicate with the world outside, in this case speaking through the natural force of gravity.   Whether it is a bookshelf masquerading as a swing or a shower curtain as a wind chime, these little games that I play with the fabric that make up a home, immediately and transparently register an authentic interaction with the world out there.   Despite living inside walls under the shadow of a roof.   And maybe by doing so, a sensitivity and meaningfulness returns, no longer masked by a slow entropy numbing unnoticed.

On the eve of a threshold into unknowns, rafters and eaves need a good shaking, since wind chimes are often missing. A string of holiday lights is about the only thing found hanging from the roof of a suburban American house.

Nov 30, 2017 01:21PM, Published by North Hills Monthly Magazine, Categories: Home+Garden, Advertisers, Today
http://www.northhillsmonthly.com/2017/11/30/161834/toying-with-gravity

Made in the USA
Middletown, DE
17 March 2023